CS
16
.M5
1977

SOCIAL SCIENCES & HISTORY DIVISION

THE CHICAGO PUBLIC LIBRARY

FORM 19

DON'T CRY "TIMBER!"

by

PRUDENCE GROFF MICHAEL

Library of Congress Catalog Card Number 78-20129

ISBN 0-9600-9321-4

Copyright © 1970 by
Prudence Groff Michael

Mrs. Ralph W. Michael
64472 U.S. 31
Lakeville, Indiana 46536

Printed in the
United States of America

First Printing — August 1970
Second Printing — October 1971
Third Printing — April 1973
Fourth Printing — January 1976
Updated Fifth Printing — June 1977
Sixth Printing - June, 1978

Dedicated to the Memory

of my dear Parents

Fred C. and Alice Groff

and their unfailing

Love and Encouragement

Contents

	Page
Chapter I—DON'T CRY "TIMBER"	7
"X" Marks the Starting Spot	8
Homework	10
Traditions: True or False?	12
No Family Bible?	12
Two Little Words	14
Chapter II—OFF WE GO!	16
Dig and Delve Material	17
County History Books	18
Points to Remember	18
Family History Books	19
L. D. S. Genealogy Services	20
Chapter III—CENSUS RECORDS	21
Some Interesting Sidelights	21
More Interesting Sidelights	23
Microfilm Reading	25
Chapter IV—COUNTY FORMATIONS AND EARLY RECORDS	27
Interesting Facts to Remember	29
Chapter V—RESEARCH IN THE ARCHIVES	32
County Courthouses	32
Wills and Land Records	35
Naturalization Records	39
W P A Records	40
State Records	40
National Archives Records—and All Sorts of Acts!	42
Hoyt Index	45
Virginia Revolutionary War Warrants	47
More Acts—and Important Information	47
Chapter VI—CHURCH RECORDS	49
Quaker Records and Others	50
W P A Checklist	53
No Marriage License?	54
What Church?	55

Chapter VII—DISSA AND DATTA 56
   Dating—Old and New Style 56
   Double Dating 57
   The Palatines 58
   Naming Systems 58
   Swiss Names 60
   Feminine Endings 60
   "X" Marks Another Spot 61
   The Pennsylvania Archives 61
   The Continental Army, Revolutionary War 63
   Sending Money to Foreign Countries 65
   Then What Happens????? 66
   "Thoughts on Lineage Research." 68
   Commonly Used Words 68

THE ENDWORD—OR BACKWORD 73

Prudence Groff Michael

I
Don't Cry "Timber!"

So you've wondered a hundred times who your great-great-Grandparents were, and how they lived! But have you really done anything constructive to find the answers? You may have a whole dresser drawer full of excuses, such as: "The family Bible records were all lost," or, "Great-Grandpa died ninety years ago, and not a soul has any information on him." It's too late to sit around now wishing you had asked your grandmother what she knew about the family—and the longer you wait to do something at this point, the harder things are going to get.

Dear Friend, take heart! Everyone left records of some sort; the only thing necessary to find answers to all—well, nearly all—your problems is a good, itching curiosity, plus the know-how to locate existing records. And if **you** supply the curiosity, this little book will go a long way to supply the know-how.

We all have family lines—this is one of Nature's laws—otherwise none of us would be here! No one ever walked through life without leaving tracks of some sort behind him, but each year those tracks have a way of becoming more dim. If you're interested in tracking down maybe two or three hundred years worth of ancestry, right now is the time to start.

Remember, "The Moving Finger writes; and having writ, Moves on."

So don't just **stand** there! Don't cry "Timber!" while your family tree comes crashing to the ground! It's up to you to save it, so roll up your sleeves and set to work.

This old world is definitely in need of family trees that will show better timber—and fewer nuts!

"Just exactly **what**," you may ask, "is genealogical research?" Be assured it is much more than a cold, matter of-fact recitation of names and dates of an ancestor. In order to make research come alive, we must always remember that these names and dates in our ancestry were connected to very real, live people—our own forebears. They possessed the same emotions of hope, fear, longing, and love that we today have. They, too, filled in a whole lifetime between their birth and death, with the same type of problems and happiness we ourselves are faced with right now. And they struggled through life with none of the wonderful comforts we of today take for granted. The chances are that not many of us today could ever have gone through the things our ancestors were confronted with.

A study of your own family line will be sure to turn up many interesting events and happenings—knowledge of which has somehow become lost through the years. Thus, those shadowy ancestors will eventually become as near and dear to you as your own immediate family. And why not? They **were** your family, many, many years ago.

Of course, in order to be a good researcher, some qualifications are necessary—but they are very simple and ordinary. There must be a **desire** to know something about your family line—for without this desire there will be no motivation to even get started. A good mind is also a necessity—otherwise how would we sort out the most obvious errors that are sure to be encountered? Next, perseverance is needed—because blank pages are sure to be drawn somewhere along the line, and many stone walls will be encountered during the research.

Desire, a good mind, and stick-to-itiveness; certainly not an overwhelming set of attributes! And the nice part about the whole business is that most of us do have these very qualifications!

"X" Marks the Starting Spot

Genealogical Research concerns individuals and their relationship to each other through succeeding generations. Webster has defined it as an account of family ancestors or relatives; the investigation of family pedigrees. And a genealogist, of course, is one who does the investigating, then puts the pieces together to form a complete picture. Accepted as one of the Social Sciences, genealogical research is now recommended as an excellent therapy for boredom or depression, and has become one of the fastest-growing hobbies in existence. More and more young people are developing an avid interest—but whatever your age, once the bug bites you, recovery is positively never guaranteed.

And if your investigation turns up an occasional witch or horse-thief somewhere along the line—who cares? It's still the cleanest fun in the country! (And if the shoe fits, I say you can always try a smaller size!)

As in other fields of research, start with what you know, then work from the known to the unknown. Using a "Pedigree Chart," which may be purchased by the dozen or the hundred from several places (including The Everton Publishers, Inc., P.O. Box 368, Logan, Utah 84321, or Bookcraft, 1848 West 2300 South, Salt Lake City, Utah 84110) fill in all the spaces you can. Start with yourself and your parents. As work continues you may not be sure about some of the names and dates, so just leave these places blank—for a while. However, you may have at least **some** data on, say, your great-great-grandparents, so put in whatever information you can, at any spot. In this way it's possible to work both ends against the middle, and eventually the whole chart will be completed.

Another chart called the "Family Group" sheet will record one individual set of parents and their children. These may also be purchased at one of the above addresses. One dozen of each type chart would be about right if you're just starting out. Two dozen would probably be even better, since the cost will be quite reasonable. Both charts are necessary if you hope to keep orderly records. They make easy work of trying to keep track of whether great-aunt Minnie was born in 1876 or 1879—and whether she was the daughter of Henry and Rebecca, or of Frederick and Keziah.

The three main stages in research development are:

    1—Home work.
    2—Library work.
    3—Archives work.

The place from which any information or proof of statement may be obtained is called the source. There are two main classes of source materials:

1—Primary records.
2—Secondary records.

A primary, or original record, is the best proof for any statement. This category includes original wills, original Bible records, marriage records, church records, etc. In other words, anything in the ORIGINAL draft. Any copy of such a record, if made by photocopy, Xerox, etc., is still considered as original, and therefore a primary record.

Secondary evidence would include books, statements and traditions passed on by anyone, tombstones (which may be either primary or secondary, depending on when the stone was placed), naturalization records (because some applicants didn't quite tell the truth, these can't always be classified as primary evidence), and other records that have been copied. Thus, a hand-copied record from a family Bible becomes a secondary record because of the human penchant to make copying errors. The information in the Bible, though, is still primary evidence.

Remember that one ambition turns up ten abilities—so keep plugging away! Most worthwhile things require at least some struggle, but the rewards are great.

Homework

1—Talk to all possible family members, friends and neighbors to see what information they might have on your early family. Write this information down as they are giving it— or get it on a tape recorder.

2—Write letters to relatives, including even some of the younger ones who might just possibly have some material you've never even heard about.

3—Search old Bible records, old letters, etc. Clean out old trunks if you're lucky enough to have some stored in your basement or attic— providing you're lucky enough to have a basement or attic! These carefully-saved **treasures might** surprise you!

4—Fill in your pedigree and family group charts as each new bit of data is discovered.

You will note that on these pedigree (or "ancestor") charts, all males have an even number, and each female has an uneven number—that of her husband plus one. The interesting thing here is that the number of ancestors doubles with each succeeding generation; by going back four generations (starting with your parents), to your great-great-grandparents, you'll have thirty direct ancestors. Six generations back will make the number 126, and ten generations back will give a grand total of 2,046 ancestors. Thus, someone born around 1900 might very possibly have sixty-four or more ancestors who served in the Revolutionary War, or who rendered patriotic service of some kind. Probably five or six generations back will place you in this era.

Ten or twelve generations are about as far back as most of us can go, unless we descend from Royalty. This is because it was not until about the twelve or thirteen-hundreds that surnames (last names) came into general usage. For English-speaking people, however, the custom of having surnames started about the mid ten-hundreds, following England's invasion by William the Conqueror, also known as the Duke of Normandy.

When writing letters don't forget that one little, stamped, self addressed envelope enclosed with your letter asking for information, can do more to create warm, good-will than a bushel of "thank yous." Sometimes, I'll grant, it seems like half of those recipients must spend most of their waking hours diligently steaming off those very stamps to swell their own collection! Unfortunately, no one as yet has come up with the exact way to meet this problem. However, for those of you who receive information request letters—or information exchange offers—please, please do make a special effort to answer, particularly when a stamp is enclosed! Write, even if all you can say is that you regret you have no information. This way the inquirer will at least know the letter has reached you, and the stamp used for its intended purpose. After all, nothing in this world quite compares to that warm, deep-down faith in fellow man being upheld!

Traditions: True or False?

Probably every family has traditions of some sort, such as:

1—Great-great-Grandpa Jones fought beside General George Washington all through the war—and once saved his life.

2—Three brothers came to America two hundred or so years ago from Germany (or England, or ????).

3—A huge inheritance, usually complete with a family castle, was supposed to have been left many years ago, somewhere in Europe. It reverted to "the Crown" before family descendants here in America could claim it.

4—Stories handed down claim there was an Indian Princess somewhere in the family. (Oddly enough, this always seems to be a Princess—and not a plain, ordinary Indian maiden!) It's amazing how many families have these tales of an Indian background, and most of such traditions can be taken with a grain of salt. The whole thing has to do with land or money bounties given by the government many years ago to persons able to prove they were of Indian descent. This was in retribution for territory taken from the Indians, earlier. Since a chief or a princess naturally was entitled to a better settlement, descendants of such persons also received more. It then became THE thing to (even jokingly) claim one had Indian ancestry in his background, and passed down through the years, such stories many times became accepted as gospel truth. Many false claims were also filed for the free handout provided by the government, but most of these couldn't provide actual proof of Indian descent.

Most of us, of course, descend from very ordinary people quite like ourselves. But what should be done about these family traditions that keep nagging at our thoughts? Often there is at least some truth in many of them, so everything should be written down exactly as told, stating who gave the data, as well as when and where it was received. State, however, this is tradition, then work to prove or disprove.

No Family Bible?

If no family Bible records exist, and no one knows a thing about your early forebears, it is still possible to trace the line through:

1—Census records.
2—Marriage records.
3—Birth and death records.
4—Probate records (wills, guardianship papers, probated estates, etc.)
5—Mortality schedules.
6—Land records (deeds, mortgages and other records often give genealogical data).
7—Genealogy queries in various magazines and newspaper columns.
8—Naturalization records.
9—Old city directories.
10—County History books, and various compiled family record books.

Each of the above, plus some other helps, will be elaborated on later. Right now get started on the following:

1—Fill out pedigree and family record charts.

2—Try to get data from all possible relatives.

3—Write letters for information—but be sure to keep each one short. Be explicit in what you want, and don't ask for too much data at one time—this is a sure way to scare someone off—particularly older people. Enclose a stamped, self-addressed envelope! Keep carbon copies of all letters you write. Save all replies received—you'll be sorry if you don't! (The letter you throw out tomorrow is sure to be the letter you want next week!)

The following is a horrible example of what **not** to do in sending off a letter, and definitely illustrates many reasons why replies are sometimes never received. This letter was actually received, with no stamp enclosed for a reply; only the names have been changed. It was addressed to an Indiana Historical Society:

> "Dear Sirs:
> I am working on my genealogy and wonder if you can help. I am looking for information on George (?) Johnson or any Johnson born on December 2, 1861 at Pembrook, Indiana. Am looking for his parents. Where they were from, and dates.
> He married Mary Brown. Could you tell me if Brown was her maiden name and where her parents are from and when born.

Also anything you might have on Henry Rich born in 1835 in Indiana or his wife Margaret born 1839 in Indiana. Don't have counties for either.

Need parents names for both, where from and where born. Thank you, Jane Doe."

Another very poor letter is this one:

"Dear Sir:
I am trying to find the name of James Lee's father. Also his mother. He was born some place in Kentucky in 1799. Do you have any records that would give the names of his parents? His date of birth might have been 1809 instead of 1799."

Both of the above constitute mighty big requests!

Two Little Words

The Greeks had two words for it—Genea, meaning descent, and logos, meaning discourse—which we may interpret to mean talk about line of descent. Nearly everybody loves to talk about his family, so don't be bashful about writing letters or asking questions. You just might strike a gold mine when it comes to reaping information!

At the library, for instance, it's considered perfectly good manners to strike up a conversation with any other researcher. You just might discover you share a common ancestor!

DON'T, however, try to hold a two hour monologue about your fascinating great-grandmother—the only person **that** interested in her was (or should have been!) your great-grandfather.

* * * * *

Then there was the teacher who told her students: "We're all here to help others." One little boy, looking very puzzled, responded: "Yes—but what are the OTHERS here for?"

* * * * *

Don't make the mistake of confusing an issue—keep in mind the **important** things you're looking for. Going off on too many irrelevant tangents will usually produce nothing but wasted hours. Things of minor consequence, however interesting in some aspects, can always be delved into at a later date. Learn to recognize what is vital and really important—far too many people make the mistake of constantly getting lost in the woods because of so many trees! Concentrate on the problems that are actually involved.

Something to remember: When exact birth dates are unknown (in trying to work out a family line of descent) it is usually safe to allow an average of about twenty-five years between each generation of males, and about twenty years between each generation of females. Thus, four generations of males and five of females will usually span a hundred years. If things work out to much less than this, then probably different lines are being intermixed. For instance, not many couples would have had children at the age of twelve or fourteen.

* * * * *

For those able to trace their family back unusually far, excellent eight, nine, and twelve generation pedigree charts may be purchased very reasonably from Bookcraft, 1848 West 2300 South, Salt Lake City, Utah 84110. Send for their catalog.

* * * * *

Once you get started, don't let a messy work table worry you. An uncluttered desk is not necessarily the result of a neat, orderly mind—it may just represent an EMPTY mind. So cheer up!

* * * * *

You'll be surprised at all the little pearls of philosophy constantly encountered in research. This astute little gem was found carved on an old, old gravestone:

"Here lies my wife, and here I lie;
At last she's at rest—and so am I."

II
Off We Go!

Now that a start has been made, you're ready to get on with the meatier aspects of tracking down those elusive ancestors! One of the very best research sources, particularly for the beginner, is the local library. Before starting on this project, though, you should check through your pedigree and family record charts to pinpoint data still lacking. Then in a large, three-ring notebook (or same size spiral type book) write down all information that must be searched for. This might include, for any particular person, name of spouse, marriage date, place of residence, war record, place of burial, and so on. It is often possible to find all these facts in various records at the library, so this makes a good beginning. However, if the above little chore isn't done ahead of time, your mind is apt to suddenly and unexplainably go blank the minute you're enfolded within the hallowed expanses of the building!

In all genealogical research one should give source of information, then either abstract or quote in full, to supply proofs for each statement. Put down the name of the book, author, publication date, publishing company, and page where statement is found. If the library has a photocopying machine it's a real timesaver to slip the book in the machine and photocopy any extensive material. Most libraries charge about ten cents a page, and many machines do an excellent job of reproducing even photographs.

Most printed Genealogies and Compendiums were compiled from information sent in by family members. Since the material was generally printed as the editor of the book received it, accuracy of statements can sometimes be questioned. Thus, any data found in books should be verified by further individual investigation, when possible, from primary sources— particularly if there seems to be discrepancies.

Informative data will probably be found in County History Books (most of which contain biographical sketches by townships), Family genealogy books, various genealogical magazines such as the "Genealogical Helper," "Pennsylvania Traveler," and so on. Old newspapers may contain obituaries, wedding reports and other news items of much interest, with many of these old newspapers very possibly having been put into microfilm form. Other sources will include County and State Archives books (such as the Pennsylvania or New Jersey Archives), DAR records of various types that through the years have been copied by members of this organization, vital statistics (such as the WPA copies to be found in some libraries), cemetery records, abstracts or indexes of warranty deeds (land records), abstracts of wills, Church records, and so on.

The Hoyt Index, available in both book and microfilm form, gives names of all Revolutionary War soldiers who ever applied for pension or bounty land. Information on the soldiers usually includes veteran's name, the state from which he served, his pension file number, and sometimes his widow's name will also be given. Other data is occasionally included. To obtain detailed information one should request form 6751, from:

>General Services Administration
>National Archives and Records Service
>Washington, D.C. 20408

The free order-form (or several) should be requested, for "Photocopies Concerning Veterans." Filled out and returned, this may bring you many pages of detailed information on your soldier ancestor, and perhaps, his family.

Dig and Delve Material

Mortality schedules, taken with the census of 1850-60-70 and 1880, gave names and other information on any household member who had died the preceding twelve months. These schedules may be found in many State Libraries and Historical Societies, with some being at the DAR Library in Washington, D.C. These schedules can be very helpful in some cases, since they were made before many states required records of deaths to be kept. More information on Mortality schedules will be found later in this book.

It's a good idea to familiarize yourself with material in your local library, however small, before going on to a large library. Don't hesitate to ask the librarian what material is available for genealogical research—she usually will be happy to help you. However, **don't** expect any librarian to compile a family tree for you—or to do any extensive research. And don't bore **anyone** with an extensive, two-hour recital of all the wonderfully fascinating history you've uncovered on your various family lines—no matter how thrilled you are with your discoveries. Not too long ago I overheard two women talking in a library; one of them said, "I can't stand being around Myra anymore. She's always so busy talking about her research findings that I never have any time to talk about mine!"

'Nuff said!

County History Books

County History Books should be checked for family sketches. Some branch of the family, of course, should have been in that particular county at the date the book was published. Biographical sketches are usually to be found at the back of these books, grouped by townships. Since a charge was always made to have family material printed—plus the fact that one then had to agree to buy at least one or more copies of the book—not all families accepted the invitation to get themselves in print. Among those who did accept, there was sometimes a tendency to more or less "gild the lily" on family write-ups. Thus, some statements might possibly have been embellished at times to make a really impressive story—but even so, the account will probably be found fairly accurate. In some instances a complete line back to the immigrant ancestor will be given—in which case you're really in luck. Remember it was not only the "best" or most important families that appeared in such books—anyone willing to pay could be included.

Points to Remember

1—Be alert for collateral lines (families into which your relatives might have married).

2—Be conscious of immigration patterns—whole groups usually came together to a new location—often fathers and several sons, brothers, uncles, cousins—and sometimes several neighbors made the move with the group. Stopovers were frequently made, lasting several months or even years. Occasionally this resulted in new settlements and villages being formed; then at least part of the group moved on.

3—Travel was difficult, even for courtship, so young men of marriageable age seldom went far for a bride in any section of the country. Usually the bride was a fairly close neighbor; look for her family to be located near that of her husband. This is particularly helpful in searching census records, which will be covered later.

4—Write down all data you find that might pertain to your family, giving book title, publisher, publication date and page number. Use plenty of space—never crowd your notes.

5—Watch for "embroidered" statements and outright errors in all material, but copy everything exactly as you find it. Later you can add your own interpretations and comments to sort of clarify things.

6—Most books have an index at either the front or back. However, all names mentioned in the book do not always get indexed, so a little close page-by-page scrutiny is sometimes a good idea.

Family History Books

Family History Books have a great amount of information—but again observe the above precautions. Be especially alert for birth dates of children; sometimes births actually figure out to be only five or six months apart! Such errors are frequently copied and recopied, thus compounding the original error. It often appears likely the compiler of the material was more interested in quantity, rather than quality, and such records sometimes can be almost worse than none at all.

Sometimes a researcher would practically give his eye-teeth to acquire a copy of a certain book that has been out of print for many years. Sometimes such books may be purchased through a used-book dealer, many of whom are scattered around the country.

One of the best ways to get such a book is by writing:
University Microfilms International
Books and Collections Dep't.
300 N. Zeeb Road — Ann Arbor, Michigan 48106

Their new service, called "Books On Demand," supplies practically any book ever printed, in either xerographic form or 35mm. roll microfilm reproduction. Moderate costs vary according to length, with microfilms costing less than books. A custom reproduction is made for each order. Write for their catalog of genealogies and family histories.

L. D. S. Genealogy Services

The Pedigree Referral Service instituted in 1963 by the Mormon Church (Latter Day Saints) to bring together those researching similar family lines, has now been replaced with the "Temple Ordinance Indexes," providing genealogical information on millons of names from three major files. These are: The Computer File Index (microfiche cards of family lines); The Temple Index Bureau; and The Family Group Records Archives.

Main purpose: to provide data previously submitted to the Mormon genealogy project. Since correctness was never verified, many errors appear — but material still can prove helpful. At present 50¢ per name research is charged for each category, regardless of whether anything is found. If search is successful, a photocopy of the most probable matching entry is supplied. Inexpensive request forms are sold through the General Church Distribution Center, 1999 West 1700 South, Salt Lake City, Utah 84104; also through local Mormon Church units. Complete form, enclose fee and mail to: The Church of Jesus Christ of Latter Day Saints, Genealogical Dep't., 50 East North Temple St., Salt Lake City, Utah 84150.

* * * * *

If no birth certificate is available for an ancestor, but he died when death certificates were mandatory, the latter will usually give names of parents, birthplace, et cetera. Request **PHOTOSTATED** copy.

III
Census Records

The taking of the first Census Record for the entire nation was approved on March 1, 1790, with enumeration to begin the first Monday in August, 1790, and end within nine months. The main object of the enumeration was to determine the number of members in the House of Representatives to which each state was entitled. Many libraries have this 1790 census in book form, giving names of household heads. Others in the household are listed within broad age-brackets, but very little other information is given. This census is probably one of the best places to start tracking down a family, if most other records are unavailable. Many libraries now have at least some census records in microfilm form. If your library has a microfilm reader, it can rent any census film you're interested in, for one dollar plus postage, from:

> The Southwestern Genealogical Library
> 3651 Douglas Avenue
> El Paso, Texas 79903.

Some Interesting Sidelights

1—Be sure to copy County, Township and page numbers from all census records. If you aren't sure of the state in which a person lived in 1790, search the index at the back of each book.

2—Existing 1790 census records include: Connecticut, Maine, Maryland, Massachusetts, New Hampshire, New York, North Carolina, Pennsylvania, Rhode Island, South Carolina, Vermont, and Virginia.

3—Partial census records for 1790 have been reconstructed mainly from tax records for the District of Columbia, Georgia, Kentucky and Virginia.

4—Be alert to all spelling variants—frequently phonetical spellings were used when recording names. Census takers often were not too well educated, and in addition to this, many people did not know for sure exactly how their own name was spelled.

5—Some states have an Index of their census records, in book form, particularly for the earlier years of sparse population. Some of these indexed records include Indiana for 1820 (complete census in book form compiled by Willard Heiss), Ohio for 1820 and 1830 (3 volumes), and Pennsylvania for 1810. There are, of course, many, many others. Check with your librarian.

6—It is generally supposed that in 1814, when the British set fire to the Capitol buildings, many of the original census records stored there were destroyed in the flames. However, the possibility seems good that at least some of these records were not even in the Capitol by that date. This thought is borne out by the resolution of Congress, approved May 28, 1830, which stated that District and Supreme Courts of the United States be directed to transmit to the Secretary of State the several returns of the enumeration of the inhabitants of the United States filed in their respective offices by direction of the several Acts of Congress, passed the first of March 1790, the 28th of February 1800, the 26th of March 1810, and the 14th of March 1820. The implication is that by 1830 the returns for the first four census enumerations had not been sent to Washington, and were, as of 1830, still in custody of officials in the judicial districts of the states.

7—In addition to tax lists being used to reconstruct the 1790 census of Virginia, some State enumerations of 1782 through 1785 were also used. Only 39 counties were included.

8—The 1790 Vermont census was actually done in 1791.

9—"Off-year" state census records were occasionally made by state governments (for some states only), generally about half-way between the Federal enumerations.

10—From 1790 through 1840 only name of household head was given in census records, with various age brackets for all household members. Some of these provided a column for occupation, number of slaves owned, etc.

11—The first census record of New Jersey still existing is that of 1830, which is, however, incomplete. The New Jersey State Library, at Trenton, houses bound volumes of New Jersey census records for the decennial years of 1855 through 1915.

12—Various counties, or parts of counties, are completely missing from at least some of the states for every census.

13—The District of Columbia (as we know it today) census for 1790 is included in the 1790 census for Maryland's Montgomery and Prince Georges Counties.

14—The 1820 and 1830 Wisconsin census records are with those of Michigan.

15—The 1860 Nevada census is included in the 1860 Utah census.

16—The 1860 schedules for the present State of Oklahoma are with those of Arkansas, which was then Indian lands.

17—The 1860 records for the present State of Wyoming are with those of Nebraska.

18—The 1860 schedules for the present State of Colorado are included in the Kansas census for that year.

More Interesting Sidelights

The 1820 census is known as "the tricky one," because of one extra column that appears. One column is headed: "Males 16 to 18," with the next column headed: "Males 16 to 26." There is no error here; the overlapping age-brackets were deliberate. The purpose was an attempt to estimate how many males would be in the military-age group for any war that might break out in the near future. One should be particularly cognizant of the overlapping ages, however, since any male between the ages of sixteen and eighteen will be listed again in the sixteen to twenty-six year bracket. Keep this in mind!

The female grouping in this same 1820 census, does not contain the sixteen to eighteen year column.

A column headed "aliens" also appears in this census, and in some cases could be very informative.

The 1830 census has, among other things, a space in which deaf, dumb, and blind persons were listed.

The 1840 census gives, in addition to the regular data, names and exact ages of War pensioners living in a household. Specific data will be found on the following page, for each pensioner. This information has also been published in book form, under the title of: "A Census of Pensioners for Revolutionary or Military Services." Some of the pensioners listed in this book are not Federal pensioners, but presumed to be State pensioners inadvertently included in the list.

The 1840 census also included the number of white persons over the age of twenty who could neither read nor write, plus other categories.

The census of 1850 is notorious for errors—both as to ages and place of birth of family members. Being the very first census to record names of all persons in the family, perhaps the census takers were a bit perturbed at having to record so much information at each stop, and inclined to some impatience and carelessness. One important, new bit of information given in this 1850 census is the State, Territory or country of birth for each individual; also whether or not he was married within the year; and the value of real estate owned.

The 1870 census states whether or not the parents of any individual were of foreign birth.

Branching out even more, the 1880 census gives street and house number of each person, postal address, relationship to the head of the family, occupation, and also place of birth of parents of each member of the household. This is the last census open for public examination. It covers data from June 1, 1879, and ends May 31, 1880. Only persons who were living on June 1, 1880, were included; no others were listed. Children born after this date were omitted—even if the census was taken several months later. But anyone who died after June 1, 1880, was included, even though death occurred prior to date the census was taken. *(1900 Census now open)*

Pay plenty attention to your senses—woops!—**census**. (On the other hand, it will probably be a good idea to pay plenty attention to both!) Sometimes you'll get a "hunch" about a thing—nothing you can really put your finger on—but follow it through, anyway. Sometimes these "hunches" lead to really big things. Of course, nothing in genealogical research ever takes the place of documented facts, but the longer you work at trying to put your family line together, the more you'll find a sort of "feeling" developing which eventually leads you to documented facts.

Use your imagination! Let yourself go! Remember good old Perry Mason, Sherlock Holmes and J. Edgar Hoover! Even a faint whiff of aroma that smells like a mystery sets their adrenal glands churning like mad, and immediately galvanizes them into action. Don't be afraid to follow your secret feelings through—often even a bad "hunch" eventually leads to something good! The main thing is: keep your mind stirred up and active. Remember the old pioneers always used to say, "Nothing ventured, nothing gained!"

Microfilm Reading

After a roll of microfilm is put on the reading machine, facilitate rapid search for a particular name by simply running down the list of surnames, rather than trying to read any of the given names while hunting for a particular family. When the correct surname is discovered, check the complete data accompanying this name, and write down all information. Be sure to include county, township and page number, as well as visitation number listed for the house. Column headings will appear at the top of each page—hopefully! Sometimes this information will be found only on the first page of a county, however.

Do not attempt to read any film while machine crank is being turned. Set microfilm at desired position, read, then turn to the next position. The librarian will be happy to initiate you into the mysteries of the proper way the reader must be operated—just ask! Crank machine with even movements. Never allow ink from ball point pens to touch the reading plate —it becomes almost impossible to remove such ink. A magnifying glass is sometimes helpful for final deciphering; the reading is often a bit difficult—but always fun and exciting! And practically nothing can equal the thrill that suddenly floods your entire body as you come across an ancestor's name, and see the actual notation that was made all those many years ago!

Unless you do your own census reading, half of the fun will be lost. Any other person, of course, relies for the most part upon information given him, then works from that. But if you read the records yourself, it's usually possible to pick up collateral lines which only you, being familiar with other names connected with the family, might recognize.

Be alert to birthplaces listed for various children in each family; this will help identify migration trails and pinpoint dates. Also, when real estate or personal value is large, this is almost a sure indication a will is on file somewhere. And keep in mind that a thousand dollars in the early days represented a lot more money than it does now!

Many libraries have a Library Loan Service—which simply means they will loan at least some of their books to another library, in any part of the country, for a stated period of time. This is particularly useful when Family History or County History genealogical books are concerned. The borrower's only cost is payment of postage, with lots of important information frequently gleaned. Many of these books are now, of course, out of print. Consult your local librarian for full details.

Remember that the designation "Junior" didn't necessarily indicate a relationship of **son** — only that a younger man of the same name lived in the vicinity.

When reading microfilms remember to "rest" your eyes occasionally by looking off into the distance. This is the sure way to prevent that "cross-eyed" feeling!

IV

County Formations and Early Records

If you've worked long and hard trying to unearth data on an early ancestor—and appear to be getting nowhere—do you sometimes feel your problems are absolutely unsolvable? Then, I urge you, relax a minute and consider that superb sleuth, Perry Mason. Like Perry, you have a big mystery on your hands—so think a minute—how would this great man solve any problem? By breaking it down into simple parts, that's how!

Actually, there is no such thing as a BIG problem: all supposedly big problems are nothing more than a bunch of little ones all stuck together. Work out these little problems one by one, fit the pieces into their proper places—and voilà—the unsolvable has finally become solved! Remember that a researcher worth his salt does **not** give up. Neither does he silently let the problem fade away. The mark of an outstanding individual is his ability to envision and carry out a worthwhile undertaking. This country grew because the pioneers had an inspired determination and fervent confidence in the future. And, as their descendants, we had just better get busy and exhibit lots of those same characteristics. So—back to our research!

Today, if you're trying to get any sort of information about anyone, probably one of the first questions becomes: "Where does he live?" So, in genealogical research, this should also be one of your first concerns.

For a person to say: "Oh, I live in Indiana," would certainly not be very specific information, since Indiana covers a pretty big territory. On the other hand, if we can give a county, township, city or street address, then we have a specific breakdown—and the problem becomes much more simple.

For early research we must know something about how and when various counties were formed, because county—and even state—lines were constantly changing. Without this knowledge, research becomes almost impossible, since many counties were divided a dozen or more times before our present set-up was finally arrived at.

One of the very good aids for county formation records is: "Research in American Genealogy," by E. Kay Kirkham, published by the Deseret Book Company, Salt Lake City, Utah.

Since so many of us had early Pennsylvania ancestors, let's use that state to explain county formations and divisions. Pennsylvania, which received its first settlers in 1632, had originally only three counties: Bucks, Chester and Philadelphia —all formed in 1682. These three covered a large amount of territory, but as population increased, the settlers needed more space, so pressed onward to the fine, fertile lands further on into the state. As more and more people arrived it became necessary to create more counties, and this was done. When the population continued to increase, the counties were then cut up into smaller areas—and these in turn were often made still smaller and smaller to form newer counties. Sometimes, parts of two or three counties were taken to make one new county. A good example of how this worked would be to start with one of the original counties, Chester, formed in 1682:

1729—Lancaster County formed from part of Chester.
1750—Cumberland County formed from part of Lancaster.
1752—Berks County formed from parts of Lancaster, Bucks and Philadelphia.
1752—Northampton County formed from part of Bucks County.
1772—Northumberland County formed from part of Lancaster, Bedford, Berks and Northampton.
1785—Dauphin County formed from part of Lancaster.
1786—Luzerne County formed from part of Northumberland.
1789—Mifflin County formed from part of Northumberland and Cumberland.
1795—Ontario County formed from part of Northumberland, but was absorbed by Lycoming County in 1812.
1800—Center County formed from part of Northumberland, Mifflin and Lycoming Counties.
1804—Clearfield County formed from part of Northumberland and Lycoming Counties.

1813—Columbia and Union Counties formed from part of Northumberland.
1850—Montour County formed from part of Columbia.
1855—Snyder County formed from part of Union.

So, even though your great-great-great-grandfather might have been born in Lancaster County in 1730—and never moved from the spot—this particular area could have been in half a dozen or more counties by the time he died. Thus, legal records for him might now be found in many different county seats. Pennsylvania, which started with three counties in 1682, had eleven by 1775, and today has a total of sixty-seven.

All the above facts apply to research in any other state. Remember, records you're interested in will be found at the court house of the county your ancestor resided in **at that particular date.**

North and South Carolina, in contrast to other states, were originally divided into "districts" rather than counties. Later on the term "county" did come into general use.

The divisions of Louisiana were designated as "Parishes."

Delaware used the term "Hundreds," instead of townships, thus: Kent County, Murderkill Hundred.

Interesting Facts to Remember

1—Maine was part of Massachusetts until 1820.

2—New Hampshire claimed Vermont until 1764.

3—Vermont was claimed by New York in 1789 and 1790.

4—Part of Rhode Island was originally Massachusetts.

5—The present boundary line between New York and Connecticut was not definitely settled until 1880.

6—From 1682 to 1775 Delaware was mostly under control of the Pennsylvania government.

7—New Hampshire was part of Massachusetts until 1679—then again from 1690 to 1692.

8—In 1880 Vermont ceded a small tract of land west of the Poultney River, to New York.

9—Prior to 1853 some New York land records were kept in Massachusetts, due to the fact that Massachusetts held the land rights, but New York held civil jurisdiction to the area. Therefore, land records prior to 1853 may be found in Massachusetts, and court records will be found in New York. Massachusetts, until 1786, claimed part of New York, and also claimed another parcel of land in the southwest corner of New York until 1853. This latter land, formerly Berkshire County, Massachusetts, then became part of Columbia County, New York.

10—The District of West Augusta was a tract of land about fifty miles in from the southwestern border of Pennsylvania; for some years prior to the Revolutionary War it was claimed by Virginia. It comprised the present Pennsylvania counties of Allegheny, Fayette, Washington, Westmoreland and Greene. Most of the records for this period will be found at Morgantown, West Virginia, listed under the District of West Augusta counties of Yohogania, Ohio, and Monongalia. Pennsylvania continued to hold court in Westmoreland County, near the present Greensburg, Pennsylvania, and all of these records still existing are now at Greensburg.

11—Part of present day Adams County, Pennsylvania (formed in 1800 from York County), was claimed by Maryland for more than seventy years before the Mason-Dixon line was established. This territory, at the time of dispute, was in Baltimore County, Maryland, and includes the area that is now Gettysburg, Pennsylvania. Many of these early records, therefore, will now be found in Maryland.

12—For about fifty years Connecticut claimed the entire northern half of Pennsylvania, and sent settlers to this part of the commonwealth. This caused considerable dispute between the two, which lasted until after the Revolutionary War ended. The State Library at Hartford, Connecticut, has papers concerning these early settlers, listed as the "Susquehanna Papers."

13—From 1775 to 1783, an area now basically Kentucky and Tennessee existed by the name of Transylvania. Continental Congress refused to recognize it as the fourteenth state, although many were hopeful it would be declared such. The northern half of the area was claimed by Virginia, and North Carolina claimed the southern half. Both states voided their deeds to the area and it went out of existence in 1783.

14—From 1675 to 1750 many New England trade ships spent the winters in the warm temperatures of the South Carolina coast. A considerable number of marriages took place during this time, between men from the ships and the girls and women of the district. Thus, many South Carolina lines also connect with those of the New England area.

15—Not much is ever heard anymore about the "lost" State of Franklin (or Frankland, as it was sometimes written). It existed for a short time in the locality of present day eastern Tennessee, western North Carolina, and the southwestern part of Virginia in the Cumberland Gap area. In January of 1781, the General Assembly of Virginia signified willingness, in a resolution passed, to cede its northwest territory for part of the new state. North Carolina, in June, 1784, passed an Act ceding its western lands, including the counties of Davidson, Greene, Sullivan and Washington—which counties are now part of Tennessee. Between the years of 1784-1788, a state government flourished, but never was officially recognized, and ceased to exist at the latter date.

*****

Most cities and villages in the state of New York have a public official known as the local historian. His duties include the collection of local history items, church and cemetery records, and other pertinent data previous to 1880. He is also required to assist anyone seeking local historical information — and just might have on file the very family material you've been trying to track down. Write the Local Historian in the town your interest centers.

V

Research In the Archives

Since the various states decide whether or not their records are to be considered public, any type of record may be open for public inspection in one state, but not necessarily in another. From the Office of the Attorney General the following statement was made: "Public Records or documents are property of the State,, or some political subdivision thereof—and **not** of the individual who happens at the moment to have them in his possession." All of which means that unless a state ruling closes public inspection of records, one individual of any specific court house cannot suddenly decide not to permit anyone to look over the records in his keeping.

Many of these records are in printed form at various libraries, including some marriage records, birth and death records, abstracts of wills, abstracted land records, and so forth, which also facilitates research.

Research may be done by mail, if desired, rather than on-the-spot, in person. Of course, half the fun is missed if correspondence has to be resorted to. Some court houses, however, do not have time to search for specific material wanted, and will refer an inquirer to a local researcher who works for a fee. Exact dates and names should be given when writing for any record, along with an inquiry as to what prices will be charged. Cost of photocopies of any document is usually very reasonable. Always include a stamped, addressed, long envelope for reply. We can't get around to all the courthouses in the country in order to do our own research!

County Courthouses

Since County Courthouses are usually most easily researched for local records, let us examine some of the material they contain. Included will be found:

1—Criminal records: (On file in books at the County Clerk's office.) Index books to this material makes research easier—and this applies to all Courthouse records.

2—Civil records: (Office of County Clerk or Register of Probate.) Included are actions for possession of property, both real and personal; for partition of property; to quiet title; foreclosures; divorces, and others.

3—Probate records: (Custodian: Judge of Probate—or sometimes Clerk's office. Different areas do not always have similar names for a particular office.) Included here will be found:
  a— Wills
  b— Petition for probate of wills
  c— Letters of administration and petitions for same
  d— Bond of executor or administrator
  e— Inventory and appraisement papers
  f— Petitions to determine heirship
  g— Decree of distribution of estate
  h— Release signed by heirs
  i— Guardianship papers, adoption proceedings, sale of real estate of intestates, antenuptial agreements, delayed birth certificates, change of names, secret marriages, and naturalization records.

4—Land records: (Office of Register of deeds—or County Recorder's office.)
  a— Deeds
  b— Mortgages
  c— Powers of attorney
  d— Liens
  e— Judgments
  f— Various documents affecting land titles
    Real estate cannot be sold to settle an estate unless all living heirs of the deceased person are located. Thus, much information is gleaned as to names of descendants and their place of residence. All heirs must sign a release; and to make things strictly legal, each spouse was also required to sign.

5—Miscellaneous records: Included are assessments and tax rolls, Coroner's files, and other. All will be found in some office at the County Court House.

6—Marriage Records: These are in custody of the County Clerk. After certain dates (which vary from state to state) these records also were filed at the State Capitol.

7—Birth and Death Certificates: Will be found at the County Health Department, which may or may not be located in the Court House. After a certain date these records were also filed at the State Capitol. Births, deaths, marriages, and divorces are spoken of as Vital Records—or Vital Statistics. It is possible to write for such data. Send all information possible, including all dates, names, place names, and so on, that you know. Name of parents is sometimes of help; also that of spouse, if the person was married. Send check or money order—no stamps, **ever**! Three very helpful little pamphlets, covering the entire United States and Outlying Areas, are as follows: "Birth and Death Records," "Marriage Records," and Divorce Records." Information includes specific state by state addresses of where these records are available, date each locality started keeping records, and price of each.

All three may be obtained for a total of $2.10 [$1.05 crossed out]; it is not necessary to enclose a stamped, addressed envelope. Send request to:

> The Superintendent of Documents
> U. S. Government Printing Office
> Washington, D.C. 20402

Allow up to several weeks for delivery. These pamphlets are really a "must" for finding out just where to write for copies of various records. It's impossible to make a better investment if you plan to write for any of these records.

An official record of every marriage is usually available in the county seat of the county where the wedding took place—subject, of course, to various things mentioned later in Chapter 6.

Birth and death records were often not too well kept in earlier days. They were usually filled out by physicians, funeral directors or others in authority, but in most states such records were not required by law until about the late eighteen or early nineteen hundreds. Exact dates vary for all states.

Divorce records or marriage annulment records are available where the event took place. In some cases records are also filed in the state vital statistics.

Full directions for sending for any type certificate are in the above pamphlets, which were compiled by the United States Department of Health, Education and Welfare Public Health Service.

Wills and Land Records

A large amount of genealogical data may often be obtained from wills and land records. Wills, of course, usually include names of family members, place of residence (and sometimes former place of residence) and often the exact date of death will be found to have been inserted later. Sons and daughters are usually listed in descending ages. Sometimes children are not mentioned by name, but simply spoken of as, "my children." This can sometimes get to be pretty frustrating —particularly if you've been counting on a will to provide names of everyone in the family! A spouse is usually mentioned by name, as: "My beloved wife, Ann Margaret," but again may simply be spoken of as: "My wife," or "my beloved wife,"— or occasionally as "my present wife." This latter frequently means she was a second or even a third or fourth wife. Remember, too, that women left wills.

Index books are on file at Courthouses, and facilitate search for wills. An approximate date of death should be known by any researcher, since each index book contains records for several years. From these index books one can refer to the book containing the exact copy of the will. Photocopies or Xerox copies of all records are usually available for a fee, for either on-the-spot research or research by correspondence.

Land records frequently provide names of parents, children and spouse of property owner, as well as place of residence and former residence (sometimes). "Bill of Sale" records are included in the deed indexes; these are important to check because they often state the next place of residence planned in a move. A "Power of attorney" letter, requesting another person to be the legal representative, contains important genealogical information usually, and should be noted in any index book.

Two indexes are to be found in the office of the Register of Deeds, for any land transaction. One, called the Grantor Index, gives name of person selling the land; the Grantee Index gives name of buyer of the land. One may sometimes be lucky enough to find a book marked, "Index to Original Tract Entries," which will contain records of the first sales of each plot of land made in a new county. Sometimes the land will be mentioned as being "patented." This is the same as being "bought," and is the same as a deed of ownership. Records may be found at times in the State capitol, also.

Guardianship or Orphan Court records are of much value because they give information on what happened to minor children after the death of either one or both parents. The Court usually appointed a guardian until such children became of legal age, and exact relationships are always spelled out in these papers. Sometimes, of course, in spite of the fact a child was orphaned, no such steps were taken, or else records have been lost.

In any index search great attention must be paid to the spelling of names. For instance, in one record I found my husband's great-grandfather, Christian Megerle, listed as Christian McErly. Possibly the guttural German pronunciation of the name accounted for the spelling by the person who did the writing, but this definitely-not-German version of the spelling took some little time to register!

On the other hand, when my great-great-great-Grandfather Jonathan Gillam applied for his Revolutionary War pension, the clerk making out the papers spelled the name three different ways—Gillam, Gillum, and Gillham. In my Pontius family line, so many different spellings appear that one soon becomes dizzy watching for them! Included spellings have been found as: Pontius, Pontis, Puntis, Pontious, Ponches, Punches, Pontzious—and about thirty other versions. My George Michael Hittle ancestor, an early Pennsylvania immigrant, has been found as Jurg Michel Heuttel, Georg Hipple, Georg Michael Hittell—and in one early census record as Georg Michael Huckle! Another common spelling was Hittler.

Sometimes a particular locality is responsible for spelling changes—a German settlement would naturally tend to use the German style of spelling, while a French settlement inclined to give their own interpretation to many names. Thus, the name "Vesqueau" became "Wesco" in a German-settled area of Pennsylvania—while the German name "Hittle" became "Hittell" in some instances. The warning, then, in any research must be: "Keep alert to all possible name spellings!"

Since, however, one of the very best proofs of family lineage is a **will**, the importance of locating one cannot be stressed too strongly. Too many people think that because their family never possessed an over-abundance of money or land, no will was ever made—so don't even attempt a search. Just don't jump to any conclusions along this line—nearly everyone a hundred or two hundred years ago left a will of some kind. It should be found on file at the Court House of the county in which the person died. Since county lines and county seats sometimes changed rather rapidly, make sure you check in the county that existed at date of death. (See E. Kay Kirkham's "Research in American Genealogy.")

For instance, if your ancestor Randolph Smith died in 1831, in what is now Roanoke County, Virginia, it would be useless to search records there, since Roanoke County was not formed until 1838. As Roanoke was made up from parts of Botetourt and Montgomery counties; one of these county seats would be the place to look.

Frequently, if the deceased also owned property in other counties or states, a copy of his will may be on file there, also.

If no will was ever made, the local court ordered an estate inventory taken—even though the estate was only a small one. Listed would be every bit of property owned by the deceased—right down to (in the case of my own ancestor, David Hittle who died in 1846) six bottles of liniment! So if you want to get into some really interesting bits of information, keep your fingers crossed and hope your ancestor died "intestate" (which means without leaving a will). Then look for an Estate Inventory record, in the Office of the County Clerk or Probate Judge, at the Court House—where both wills and estate inventories are kept. Included will probably be a Bill of Sale record for the entire estate—which is simply a record of each item sold at the following Public Auction—giving the price each item brought, plus the name of each buyer. Talk about fascinating reading! You can imagine the thrill I felt in going over the Inventory and the Bill of Sale for my above David Hittle, which noted such delectable items as:

One pare of steers	$15.00
A lot of cups and saucers	.12½
A lot of plaits	.18¾
One pair of Sponmoles	2.00
One Spinningwheel	2.50
(and wouldn't I have loved that!)	
One saucage horn	.25
Six vials of linament	1.50
One twohorse wagon	27.00
One pair of Spreaders	1.00
Two jugs	.50
One Skellet	.50
One pair of candle moles	.50
One coffy mill	.25
One smoothing iron	.06
One pair of Stilliards	.75
Six meal bags	3.00
One cow	8.00
One chest	1.50
One pot trammel	.50

Most people today have never even heard of some of these items! Yet all were in common usage back in 1846—when life was much harder than it is today. I was much interested in finding out what "one pair of Stilliards" could possibly have been. After asking a number of people, the mystery was finally solved by an elderly gentleman neighbor who said this was an early form of weighing scales, consisting of a long, notched bar, with weights to hang on one end. The other end supported the article being weighed, with the weights being moved back and forth to balance.

In the records I found that David Hittle's widow, Hannah, had reserved some of the articles for her own use, and these were all itemized in a separate list. (Among other things, she kept the candle molds and smoothing iron—but not the spinning wheel!)

It was usually customary to have relatives sign a will as witnesses. Frequently one of the witnesses would be a relative of the husband, with the other being a relative of the wife. More often than not the executor was also a relative of some sort.

Naturalization Records

Until quite recently, no naturalization documents could be copied in full or reproduced in any way. But on December 5, 1972, this mandate was changed and now all documents may be reproduced in any manner desired. Only uncertified copies, however, may be provided. Records usually include date and place of birth and of arrival in this country, names of witnesses, plus date and place of procedures.

There were actually four steps involved:

1—Declaration of intention, plus other documentation connected with first papers.

2—Petition, Oaths of Allegiance, witnesses' testimony, and Proofs of Residence.

3—Court orders to grant citizenship, Certifications of Naturalization and certificate stubs.

4—Journal or Docket records kept by court.

Since the Court order (No. 3) was a matter of legal record, this is the document most likely to remain in existence today. It should be found at the court of issuance. Sometimes no separate filing is kept for naturalization material, so it occasionally may be mixed in with general court records.

Many of the older naturalization records are at the National Archives Building, Washington, D. C., or at various Federal Records Centers. Some early records, through the years, have been turned over to local historical societies for various reasons. Other places to search include police and city courts, city halls, et cetera.

The four most logical holdings are: 1—United States Courts; 2—Federal Records Centers; 3—State Archives (or Agencies); 4—County Courthouses.

For free list of Federal Records
Centers addresses write:
General Services Administration
Washington, D.C. 20408

For any material desired, contact the clerk of either the county or federal court, or the Federal Records Center of any particular area. A great number of records dating prior to September 27, 1906, are now stored in the 15 Federal Records Centers throughout the United States. Write: 'The Chief, Archives Branch' of any specific Regional Center, giving proper identification of material wanted. A small fee will be charged for reproduction of papers.

Prior to the Revolutionary War, European people settling in this country could, if they so desired, and met certain requirements, become a citizen of any one colony here. By 1776 any white person of European descent who had been born in the colonies and was loyal to our cause, became a citizen without further ado. Not until 1778, however, was this person considered a citizen of all the states. Loyal indentured servants living here during the Revolutionary War automatically became citizens.

The 1820 and 1830 census records may be of some help in determining naturalization date since both contain a column designating aliens. The 1870 census indicates if parents were foreign born. The 1880 census gives birthplace of each person, plus birthplace of their parents, which also can prove helpful.

W P A Records

1935-36 the Work Progress Administration (W P A) in many states compiled a Historical Records Survey to provide employment for various unemployed clerical and professional people during the depression. Various unpublished statistical and historical records were copied, which were then put into book form, making them more accessible to researchers. Many of these pre-date the record keeping of a state and are thus extremely helpful to genealogists. All states participated except Connecticut, Delaware, Maine, Maryland, Ohio, Pennsylvania, Vermont, Virginia and South Carolina. Libraries usually catalogue these records under "Inventory" or "Guide" to Vital Statistics, Public or Church Records. Even the smaller libraries often have copies on their shelves, especially for their own county.

State Records

State Records, including some Territorial Records, will be found at the State Capitol. Some of the things included are:

1—Land grants, militia rolls and tax lists

2—Naturalization records (see previous detailed explanation)

3—Later Vital Records (will duplicate records found in various counties)

4—Mortality Schedules of 1850, 1860, 1870, and 1880. These were recorded at the same time the census for those years was taken. An extra form was filled out at the time the census was taken, and included name of any person who had died in the twelve months previous—as of June 1. Recorded was name, cause of death, length of illness, age at death, date of death, and state or country of birth. The real purpose was that of an over-all public health record, and thirteen percent of the deaths of that thirty year period were listed in this manner. Since these Mortality Schedules predate many vital records, they can be very helpful in some cases. They were held by the United States Government for many years, then finally Congress authorized their return to the individual states.

Not all states, however, wanted them back. The National Society Daughters of the American Revolution offered a home for all schedules not wanted by a state, and this was authorized by the Director of Census. Quite a few states welcomed their records back, and these are now in depositories such as State Library, State Historical Society, or State Archives. A checklist for each state will be found in E. Kay Kirkham's, "The A B C's of American Genealogical Research."

5—Territorial Records include petitions sent by inhabitants of the various territories before they became a state, stating their complaints of various grievances, to the United States government. A long list of signers was attached to each petition, and since practically every inhabitant of a locality signed at least one of these papers—and sometimes several—this formed virtually a census record in itself for the period. Territorial Papers have been published for many areas, including the Northwest Territory; also for these states that were originally in the various Territories: Alabama, Arkansas, Florida, Illinois, Louisiana, Michigan, Mississippi, Missouri, Ohio, Tennessee, and Wisconsin.

State records start with the admission of a state to the Union. Each state has an exact record of its county boundary changes, and this is usually obtainable from any State Library.

These records will undoubtedly be more correct than any others, since each state naturally kept exact records of their county formations.

National Archives Records and All Sorts of Acts.

These are the records of the Federal Government—compiled legal or administrative needs of various originating agencies. They are noncurrent records, dating from times of the Continental Congresses, and consist of records from Congress, the courts, and various executive departments and independent agencies. The records relate to many great events in the history of our country; wihle not primarily gathered for genealogical purposes, they do contain a wealth of material for the researcher. In care of the National Archives and Records Service, Washington, D.C. 20408, if detailed information is given, this division will make a concerted attempt to find records on any person in the pertinent holdings. They do not trace lineage or construct family trees. Carefully selected records having a wide research value have been undergoing microfilming since 1940, and the process continues.

Charges for photocopies are most modest, and money is to be sent later on, when bill is received. Some records require a special order form, available on request, while a letter stating what is desired, is all that's necessary in other cases. Either photocopies of various records may be obtained, or whole rolls of microfilm. Some of the material available is:

1—Census records for the entire country, beginning with 1790. Microfilms available for any particular area.

2—Land records (including Military Bounty Land Warrants granted soldiers of some wars, for their services.) Also private land claims. Under the Acts of 1788, 1799, 1803 and 1806, a Major-General was granted 1,100 acres of land; a Captain, 300; a Lieutenant, 200; and an Ensign, 150. One hundred acres was available for a Private. Such lands were known as "Bounty Lands," and were, of course, sort of an extra payment for service to the country in time of war.

Non-commissioned officers and soldiers who enlisted for five years in the War of 1812 (unless discharged sooner) were covered by the Act of December 24, 1811. The amount of acreage was increased in the Act of December 10, 1814, for non-commissioned officers and soldiers who enlisted for the war after that date.

Later Acts made provision for men who served in other wars. The Act of March 3, 1855, provided bounty lands for non-commissioned officers and privates who had served at least 14 days in a battle in any war of the United States from 1790 to that date. It also provided for any Revolutionary War soldier who had received less than 160 acres of land under any of the former Acts.

These grants accounted for the change of residence of many soldiers as they claimed their grants, and added considerably to the westward movements in the early days of our country.

3—Indian Records. These date mostly from 1830-1940. They are primarily for the Indians who maintained their tribal status. Records include lists relating to Indian removal; annuity pay rolls; annual census rolls; estate files; Eastern Cherokee claims; and Carlisle Indian School files. Records on Indian removal are primarily on the Cherokees, Chickasawas, Choctaws, Creeks and Seminoles, dating generally from 1830 to 1852. Some records give only the names of the heads of families; others give the number of family members in each age and sex group, and for some tribes that were moved westward, original place of residence is given. The estate files are made up of wills, reports on heirship, and similar records; they date from 1907, are arranged by jurisdiction, file number and date. Card indexes are in the Bureau of Indian Affairs. Records will give for each decedent name, tribe, place of residence, date of death, and age. Other information is usually included if a report on heirship is filed. These records give name of the spouse, date of marriage, names of brothers, sisters, and children, as well as names and date of marriage of parents.

4—Ship's Passenger records, giving name, occupation of individual, name of ship, port of embarkation and arrival, and dates. Only a few records are available prior to 1820. Many gaps are found from 1820 through 1945. Some records have been destroyed by fire and others, if still in existence, have never been transferred to the National Archives.

Passenger arrivals were not required to be kept during the nineteenth century for persons entering the United States by land from Mexico and Canada. Some records of arrivals are originals, some are copies and abstracts, and some are State Department transcripts. Customs lists of aliens are also available (not complete) as well as immigration passenger lists. Because of complications in arrangement, filing system, and gaps in records, research is easier if the following is known: name of port of entry, name of ship, and approximate date of arrival. Port of embarkation, if known, will also be helpful.

5—Military service records. These date beginning with 1775, but are not complete because of many Revolutionary War and other records being destroyed by fires in Washington, D. C., November 8, 1800 and August 24, 1814. Records on enlisted men of the Regular Army include enlistment papers, registers of enlistments, muster rolls, records collected by the Adjutant General's Office, compiled military service records, and others. Some data is also on file concerning Civil War draft records, soldier burials, and records of births, marriages, and civilian deaths at army posts from 1884 to 1912.

6—Pension records. Some states paid a pension to invalid soldiers prior to 1790. After an Act dated September 29, 1789, the Federal Government took over temporarily (and later permanently) the payments for these invalid pensioners. Under an Act of March 23, 1792, as amended, other veterans could apply for pensions if they were invalids. Many of these applications were destroyed in a fire that struck the War Department on November 8, 1800, but duplicates of some reports concerning the applications are still in the War Department files at Washington, in many cases. These various Acts of Congress were known as "The Old Invalid Acts." The Act of 1818, passed by Federal law, was for soldiers not disabled. A minimum of nine months service, plus need of pension had to be proved, and only men who had served in the Continental Army and Navy were included. By 1820 more than eight thousand applications were received, resulting in the Act of Congress which required a court statement of estate and income of a veteran to prove his need of assistance. Following this, many were dropped from the list—some being reluctant to expose their lack of worldly goods, others because they could not meet the requirement of being financially indigent.

The Act of 1832, the first to include volunteers and militia men, required six months service, with no financial need necessary. By the Act of July 4, 1836, widows could apply for pension or land grant—but had to supply proof they had married before the end of the Revolutionary War. These papers give much genealogical data, including date and place of marriage, names and birthdates of children, and other information. Frequently a widow tore such pages from the family Bible and sent them on to Washington as proof.

This was followed by pensions for widows who had married at a later date. It was not until the Act of February 3, 1853, that pensions were allowed widows regardless of the date of marriage. Some documents have been transferred to the Library of Congress since an Act approved in 1903.

"Hoyt Index"

The "Hoyt Index" (both in book and microfilm form) is an alphabetical name index to the Federal Revolutionary War pension application list, Bounty Land Warrants, and Military Record files. It also includes widows who made applications for grants. Many libraries have this Index—or can obtain from the National Archives. Each application received a number, and each number was preceded by one of three explanatory letters: S, R, or W.

The letter "S" meant that the soldier himself applied for the pension or Bounty Land Warrant (Blwt.). The letter "R" meant the soldier applied, but for some reason the application was rejected because at least one of the requirements specified in the particular Act of that day, was not met. Things that could cause the application to be rejected included evidence of service, length of service, property eligibility not according to law, or service was not in the Continental Army or Navy—a requirement at a certain date. Many pensioner names listed in the "Census of 1840" included those who received state (not Federal) pensions as members of the State Militia, State Troops or "Line," and so, of course, will not be found in the Hoyt Index for Revolutionary War Pensions. A rejected application does not indicate no service for the person in question, but merely that he did not qualify at that particular date. By the time many of these men would have met the necessary stipulations, they were deceased.

A Navy pension fund was set up in 1799, following the establishment of the Department of the Navy on April 30, 1798.

No Confederate soldiers received a Federal pension; some of the states however, did grant them. (This, of course, concerns Civil War service).

There has never been a published general listing of pensioners of Wars other than the Revolution. There were 52,504 Revolutionary War survivors pensioned, and 22,644 widows received pension or land grants. The pension application files in the National Archives number in the millions. The most important categories are:

1—Revolutionary War Invalid series
2—Revolutionary War Service series
3—Old Wars series
4—War of 1812 series
5—Mexican War series
6—Civil War and Later series
7—Indian Wars series

There is also a Remarried Widows index, starting with the War of 1812. This information, on 3x5 cards, is arranged alphabetically by the remarried name, but gives name of the veteran who was her former husband, the unit with which he served, and his file or certificate number.

On May 6, 1812, Congress passed an Act whereby a noncommissioned officer or soldier could claim bounty land in one of three districts, containing a total of 6,000,000 acres. This land was in what is today Arkansas, Illinois, and Missouri. Each soldier was entitled to 160 acres, with the exception of a few men who received double bounty according to an Act passed December 10, 1814. Recipients must have served in the Regular

Army for the duration of the War of 1812. Records are in individual files, numerically arranged in two series, according to whether 160 or 320 acres were granted.

Virginia Revolutionary War Warrants

These Warrants were originally issued for service in the Continental Line of Virginia, and specified land on the south side of the Green River in Kentucky, which today is located in Virginia, West Virginia, and Kentucky. By an Act approved by Congress on June 9, 1794, holders of these warrants could surrender them for tracts of land in an area located in the Northwest Territory. This new land was known as the Virginia Military District of Ohio, and was located between the Scioto and the Little Miami Rivers. Entry papers are for the most part between 1795 and 1830, indexed in one book titled "Virginia Military Warrants, Continental Line, Alphabetical Index to Warrantees, volume 30." Rank and record of service is given, date warrant was issued, and sometimes name of heir is included. Records are held by the Bureau of Land Management, Washington, D.C. 20025.

More Acts—and Important Information

The Acts of 1850 and 1853 granted bounty land to many veterans of the War of 1812, some of the Indian Wars, and the Patriot's War of 1838—a skirmish of the New York border.

The National Archives, Washington, D.C., puts out Form 6751, which may be written for, filled out, and returned (small fee later) for photocopies of any records held concerning veterans. The Archives may be visited if personal research is desired, and this, of course, gives one the chance to examine many other records. Request forms for records by mail may be obtained free from:

> The National Archives and Records Service
> General Services Administration
> Washington, D. C. 20408

All possible bits of information should be included when filling out the form, to identify the particular person. If no data is on file, no payment requested. Fair enough! (Ask for "Order for Photocopies Concerning Veterans.")

Private land claims were grants to land that was settled before the United States acquired sovereignty to it. Included in this classification is land in the United States that was granted or settled while this country was under the rule of Great Britain, France, Spain and Mexico, between the dates of 1685 and 1853. Considerable genealogical data will sometimes be found in these records, which are incomplete. Land in various parts of the following states is included: Alabama, Arizona, Arkansas, Calfornia, Colorado, Florida, Illinois, Indiana, Iowa, Louisiana, Michigan, Mississippi, Missouri, New Mexico and Wisconsin. All land was originally part of early Territorial areas. Records are held by The National Archives and by The Bureau of Land Management, Washington, D.C. 20025. They are indexed. Research, however, is usually difficult; generally the approximate date of grant and location of the land is necessary.

A pre-emption application was a device by which a person already settled on unappropriated land made application to buy it at the minimum price. "Squatters" was the term frequently used to describe those on the land.

Many people received a quarter section of land in the "Homestead Act of 1862," after having resided on the property for a specified number of years, cultivated ten percent of the land, and having built a home of some kind on the property. While the time requirement before filing for ownership at first was seven years, by 1912 this was reduced to three years. Many Civil War veterans received land under this Homestead Act.

The National Archives has records beginning with 1775. Earlier records are in possession of the individual Colonies and Great Britain.

VI

Church Records

In America, Church Records usually antedate vital records by about two hundred years. Many New England towns kept vital records as early as the sixteen hundreds; some states kept such records for short periods of time—albeit in a rather hit-and-miss fashion. But nearly all early churches kept a record of marriages and baptisms, and usually some account of death of church members was made. Many have, through the years, been lost or destroyed, but the existing ones are usually to be found in custody of the church clerk, minister, or some other person connected with the church in an official capacity. A central registry is maintained by a few denominations, and some of these records have been published in book form or put on microfilms. When most of the midwest and southern part of our country was still a wilderness, Methodist "Circuit Riders" and Baptist "Gospel Rangers" traveled through a set circuit of the countryside, to bring the Gospel to the inhabitants scattered along the way. They traveled by horseback, becoming welcomed and honored houseguests of the people along the circuit. Sermons were preached, usually in cabins of the settlers, or out in the open air under the tall trees; funeral orations were preached for the dead—many of whom had died and were buried months before the rider or ranger arrived on that particular round. Such funeral sermons were known to have lasted a couple hours; with flowery praises extolling all possible virtues of the deceased these orations were definitely something to look forward to—and were always well attended. The circuit riders kept their own records on scraps of paper or small notebooks, and of course most of them have long since been lost forever. Thus, today it is impossible, in some cases, to ever find a record of some of these earlier baptisms, marriages and deaths.

In the areas ministered to by a "Circuit Rider," or "Traveling Preacher," a considerable amount of time usually elapsed between visits, due to weather, size of territory covered, and other circumstances. This circuit riding idea had been originated by John Wesley in England, in order to best get his religious movement before a large number of people. Although started in England in 1739, Methodism was not introduced into the American Colonies until around 1764, by circuit rider Robert Strawbridge, who came to Maryland. At about the same date Philip Embury settled in New York as a circuit rider.

Francis Asbury, in 1771, became the leader of the movement and remained as such until his death in 1816. Wesley actively supported the policies of King George III, and this caused some complications for the Methodist Society during the Revolution, resulting in the persecution of several of the Maryland and Virginia preachers.

Asbury was chosen bishop of the Methodist Episcopal Church at its formation in Baltimore, during an eleven day meeting beginning Christmas week, 1784. By the end of the war there were about one hundred circuit riders in the United States. None of them, however, were ordained ministers prior to 1784. Each of the riders frequently had as many as thirty preaching places, with salary at first being sixty-four dollars a year; by 1800 this was raised to one hundred dollars.

One of the more prominent riders in Illinois, Indiana, Kentucky, Ohio and Tennessee was Peter Cartwright. Other religious bodies, on a more limited basis, put the circuit rider system into effect during the early days—the foremost of these being the Cumberland Presbyterians.

The Wisconsin Historical Society, located at Madison, Wisconsin, has a collection of notebooks of one of these preachers, all filled with fascinating and informative bits of information concerning his journeys. His name was Draper, and he served as an itinerant minister to the people of southern Illinois, Kentucky, North and South Carolina, Tennessee, and Virginia. Some of these "Draper Papers" are now printed in book form.

Quaker Records and Others

Quaker records are abundant and were kept from 1650, the founding date of the organization in England. Organized as the

"Society of Friends," all members were placed on one spiritual level, with no priests or ministers. From the very beginning they have kept detailed records, some genealogical records covering ten and twelve generations. Their Monthly Meeting records are of particular interest, including birth, marriage and death records, as well as notations of members being received into the Society, and records of removal and disownments. These records of disownment ended all records of a person as far as Quaker records were concerned.

At a Quaker wedding all guests signed as witnesses, with the immediate family of the bride and groom signing at the lower right hand corner of the marriage record.

Today, one-third of the Quaker population of the United States will be found residing in the state of Indiana—mostly in the southern section of the state.

Many of the old records are still in various meeting houses, but some have been compiled in book form. Of particular note is "The Encyclopaedia of American Quaker Genealogy," published by the Friends Book and Supply House, Richmond, Indiana, containing records from North Carolina, New Jersey, Pennsylvania, New York City, Long Island, Virginia, Ohio and Pennsylvania. Swarthmore College, Swarthmore, Pennsylvania, also has a large file of nearly 300,000 cards and is alphabetized. Called the "William Wade Hinshaw Index to Quaker Meeting Records," this provides a great amount of genealogical information. The Department of Records, 302 Arch Street, Philadelphia, Pennsylvania, also has on deposit many Quaker records for New Jersey and Pennsylvania areas.

Baptist Church records almost never give the age of a person baptized, or even names of parents. Very few Baptist marriages were ever recorded.

Many early Lutheran and Reformed Church records for various areas of Pennsylvania are on microfilm at The Evangelical and Reformed Historical Society, Philip Schaff Library,

Lancaster Theological Seminary, 555 W. James Street, Lancaster, Pennsylvania 17603. Small areas of Virginia and New Jersey are also included. Some of these microfilms date back to the early seventeen hundreds, and record baptisms, marriages, deaths and other important data. Many old cemetery inscriptions are included. Some of the microfilms will be loaned but specific areas must be requested, and rolls are numbered. Dr. Herbert B. Anstaett is the Archivist.

The Lutheran Theological Seminary Library, 7301 Germantown Avenue, Philadelphia, Pennsylvania, also holds a number of Lutheran Church records.

Moravian records may be found at the Moravian Historical Society, Bethlehem, Pennsylvania. The Moravian Provincial Archives, Winston-Salem, North Carolina, has much material concerning the Southern Province. Material covering the eighteenth and nineteenth century Moravians in America is abundant.

Protestant Episcopal data for the United States is at The Church Historical Society of the Protestant Episcopal Church, 406 Rathervue Place, Austin, Texas. There are also many other depositories, including the Connecticut State Library, Hartford, Connecticut, which has a fine collection of Connecticut records of this church.

Mormon Archives are at the Genealogical Society of the Church of Jesus Christ of the Latter Day Saints, 80 N. Main Street, Salt Lake City, Utah.

There are, of course, hundreds of other depositories all over the country, which include most denominations. Church records will contain information on births, christenings, baptisms, confirmations, marriages, and burials. Sometimes other records are included, such as contributions, donations, and various interesting items concerned with church activities.

If you know one of your ancestors was buried in a certain cemetery, sometimes it is possible to obtain needed information on dates of birth and death—and also names and pertinent data on other family members who might also be buried nearby—by writing the minister of that particular church. Ministers are often willing to help. They usually are more than willing to check old record books for information on their early church members, and, if necessary, can turn such search over to another church member. If any extensive amount of search will be involved, you should offer some payment—or if this is refused, a small contribution to the church fund would not be amiss.

Often the minister of any church can tell you where earliest records may be found if they are no longer in his possession. Many churches not now in existence have placed their records in nearby historical societies and public libraries. Sometimes a pastor took his own records with him when he moved to another charge; occasionally these have been kept in the family and are now held by descendants, carefully preserved. The big catch here, of course, is to locate such a descendant! Perseverance, in many cases, does pay off, though, and more than one early record has been tracked down in this very manner. Other depositories for early church records include Theological Seminaries and Church Foundations.

Dutch churches scrupulously kept and preserved all their records, but since these were considered the Pastor's private property they usually went with him when he moved on to another charge. In Holland the early Dutch Law of Marriage had specifically stated that no marriage banns be granted young men under the age of twenty-five, or to young women under twenty. In addition to this the consent of the parents had to be not only given—but proved. If the couple met age specifications, the parents were obligated to consent—or show good reasons for their refusal. Consent of guardians or relatives, other than parents, was never required.

W P A Checklist

The "Check List of Historical Records Survey Publication," on the shelves of many libraries, can furnish guidance to various church record depositories located throughout the entire country, providing that particular state participated in the compilation. Twenty-seven states actually participated in the survey of vital records, and forty-three states took part in general record surveys of their counties.

Recently E. Kay Kirkham published two volumes on, "Survey of American Church Records." Volume I contains bibliographies of church records available for the major denominations east of the Mississippi River, prior to the Civil War. Volume 2 includes minor church denominations, religious migrations in the United States, and other interesting material. Both are available from the "Everton Publishers, P.O. Box 368, Logan, Utah 84321."

No Marriage License?

In the early days of our country a marriage license was not always required, which accounts for the fact that in many cases one cannot be found. There were three different methods that could be used by a couple planning to wed, and any one was perfectly valid. These were:

1—Purchase a marriage license—which was costly, and prejudiced many.

2—Have Church banns read on three successive Sundays. Sometimes these banns were tacked on the church door, thus giving notice to all who passed.

3—Obtain a Marriage Bond. This was an agreement between the groom (or someone acting for him) and a male representative of the bride (usually her father or brother) that there was no reason the marriage should not take place. Such bonds were frequently drawn up by a Justice of the Peace, and since his records were usually not made public, many cannot now be found. Even if the Justice of the Peace married the couple, it still was not mandatory that he report the ceremony. These Justice of the Peace marriages were very popular, especially in areas of few church organizations.

What Church?

If your early ancestors were Scotch-Irish, the chances are good they were members i the Presbyterian Church or the Quaker group. Most of the Irish were Catholics. As a usual rule the English people were members of the Church of England, Congregationalists, or Methodists.

Many people of German nationality were members of either the Lutheran or the German Reformed and Evangelical churches. Most Swedish people, also, belonged to the Lutheran Church.

Most of the Dutch remained true to the Dutch Reformed Church.

From the first settlement made in Connecticut in 1635, to about 1705, the only organized church in the entire state was the Congregational. Then, at this latter date, a Baptist society was formed, the nucleus of a second religious denomination. In 1789 the Methodists organized their first society in the state.

Many of the Swiss were Mennonites who came to America for religious freedom, some of whom had originally fled Switzerland to Germany. These people had an extremely hard time in Switzerland, where they were viciously persecuted in the seventeenth century. The Mennonites or Pietists (so called because of the piety for which they were noted,) because of their religious beliefs were frequently beaten, stripped of all property, thrown in irons, and many times were starved to death or beheaded. The last beheading for religious convictions in Switzerland was that of a Mennonite Preacher, Hans Landis, whose death was reported by a preacher at Zurich, in a letter dated July, 1659.

The "sign" of the Methodists was the upraised hand with the index finger pointing toward heaven. When you see this engraving on a tombstone you can be sure one who embraced the Methodist faith is buried at that particular spot.

VII
Dissa And Datta

Dating—Old and New Style

Regardless of how this heading sounds, all **dates** are confined entirely to those of the calendar! Because of the way in which the Julian calendar (used in Europe in the Middle Ages) was set up, about three days of sun time were gained every four hundred years. So by 1582 the calendar in use was actually ten days behind true time.

At this point the Gregorian calendar went into use by Roman Catholics. It had been worked out by a brother of Pope Gregory, and after his death was presented by the Pope. The Greek Church, however, stayed with the Julian calendar until World War I, so by that time their calendar was actually thirteen days behind the rest of the world.

Great Britain and the British Colonies, after an Act of Parliament, adopted the Gregorian Calendar in 1751. Naturally, a bit more time had been lost by then from actual sun time, so their old calendar was, at that date, eleven days behind. The change-over became effective in September 1752, and what ordinarily would have been the third of September officially became the fourteenth of September, 1752. Thus, the calendar caught up with actual sun time, making both once again harmonious.

Any child born on September 2, 1752, because of the change-over became twelve days old the following day when the new style dating went into effect, since eleven days had to be added to his actual age. Every person born between February 29, 1700, and September 2, 1752, became eleven days older by the new calendar. Those born before February 29, 1700, became only ten days older, since the old style calendar had a leap year date which made up one of the days not counted in the new style one.

Some chaos and confusion resulted, but most of the English people, including those in the American Colonies, immediately set their original date of birth ahead by eleven days in order to make it conform to the new calendar. (In other words, if the new style calendar had been in effect earlier, this would have been the date of their birth.)

Double-Dating

(Here, again, you can't depend on how anything **sounds!**)

Double-dating, also, concerns merely the calendar. For a period of 170 years, between 1582 and 1752, this system was in effect. In France and England, from the time of Charles IX of France, the historical year was reckoned as beginning on January first—but the legal and ecclesiastical year began on March 25th.

Thus, for instance, February 3, 1628, could be either 1628 or 1629—depending on whether it was figured with the year starting in January or March. So it became a common practice to list **both** years, in order to make sure there would be no misunderstanding, and this was spoken of as double-dating. The above date, therefore, came to be written February 3, 1628/9— or February 3, 1628/29. (In other words, it was still 1628 if time was reckoned by the old Julian calendar, but 1629 if the new Gregorian calendar was being used.)

What really was in question here was the actual date of New Year's day, since by one calendar this was considered to be March 25, but was January 1, by the other. Thus, only the dates between January 1 and March 24 are ever concerned in figuring the year an event took place—and only the years between 1582 and 1752 need be taken into account.

Since the old Julian calendar considered March the first month of the year, it must be remembered that in this case the "second" month of the year would then have been April, and not February. This must be taken into account when old records state an event happened in, say, "the third month of the year," since this could have meant either March or May!

The Palatines

Many early settlers in what is now the Lower Jordan Valley of Lehigh County, Pennsylvania, came from the Palatinate area of Germany. This was a province of the kingdom of Bavaria, lying west of the Rhine river. On the north it was bounded by the Prussian Rhine province, and the Hessian province of Rhein-Hessen. On the east the boundary was Baden, with the Rhine separating the two. The south boundary was the province of Alsace-Lorraine, with the administrative districts of Trier and Coblenz forming the western boundaries The entire area covered 2,288 square miles.

A "Palatinate" was any district ruled by a Count Palatinate, who was a royal official selected by the Emperor or King, to administer the outlying province. The people who emigrated from this area were mainly exceptionally good farmers, with generations of successful farming experience behind them. Many were descended from families who had fled Switzerland years before, because of religious persecution of some form. Since they were not allowed to own land of their own in the Palatinate area of Germany, they were anxious to emigrate and find a land where they could once again be their own master, and own fertile farmland. The answer to their prayers was Pennsylvania; they arrived in the Lower Jordan Valley over a period of years, beginning about 1732. Some Palatines, however, came as early as 1709—mostly to New York—with a few eventually trickling into Maryland and North Carolina.

While the main reason for the Palatinate surge to America was probably the desire to be their own masters, contributing factors were war and religious tyranny.

Naming Systems

Two systems of naming children were popular in the early days of our country—the Dutch system, and the German system. When thoroughly understood this frequently provides the means by which different groups of names may be fitted into the proper family, correct parents ascribed, and so forth.

Many other nationalities in this country adopted the two naming systems—particularly if residence was in an area where such systems were used—so this is not a reliable guide as to nationality of any family. Sometimes, however, it's possible to go one further generation back in research, and from a baby's name figure out who his grandparents might possibly have been.

The Dutch system named the first son for his paternal grandfather, with the second son then being named for his maternal grandfather. By this system the first daughter in a family was named for her maternal grandmother, and the second daughter was given the name of her paternal grandmother. At times it's possible to pinpoint names of all four grandparents through this old Dutch system of naming children in any given family.

The German system, particularly popular among the Pennsylvania Dutch and Palatines, was somewhat different. When this was used, a child was always given a first and a middle name—with the first name frequently being that of the father (in case a son was born), and the middle name being the given name of the baby's baptismal sponsor. In the event the baby was a girl, she was given the name of her mother, plus the name of her female baptismal sponsor. Usually a man and his wife acted as sponsors, but sometimes two unmarried people were selected. Sponsors could be either relatives or friends; sometimes the parents, themselves, acted as sponsors.

According to this system, things can sometimes get pretty complicated for the researcher. If, for instance, the father's name was George, several of the sons in turn might be given this name, plus the name of the baptismal sponsor, thus: George John, George Henry, George Frederick, and George Michael. Daughters might be listed as: Mary Anna, Mary Nancy, and Mary Elizabeth. It was generally the custom (to avoid confusion!) to call these children by their middle name. Then usually, as the children grew up, the first name was dropped for most purposes. Confusion was often compounded, however, (in the George John, George Henry, etc. example) when somewhere along the line another son might have been named just plain George.

Swiss Names

Among the Swiss settlers it was frequently common to prefix "Hans" (John) before given names for boys. The prefix "Anna" was used in the case of girls. In this case there was no set pattern for a middle name.

Many variations of any Christian name were used, such as Elspeth or Elsbeth for Elizabeth; Frid, Fridrich or Fridlin for Frederick; Christen for Christian; Madle and Madalena for Magdalena; Stoffel, Christof or Christoffel for Christopher; Hans and Johannes for John; Linert, Lieni and Leonhart for Leonard; Heinrich and Heini for Henry; and Joggi, Jakob or Jacobus for Jacob.

As may be seen, spellings varied greatly in names—not only after settling in America, but even in old records prior to that time. The letters "p" and "k" were frequently interchanged—also letters "d" and "t"; "f" and "v"; "ts" or "tz" and "z"; "ph" "pf" and "ff"; as well as "ck" and "k"; and "ch" and "k."

Feminine Endings

Variations in surname endings can often become most confusing. While it is quite well known that Polish people used the feminine ending "a," on last names, thus: Wegenska instead of the masculine form Wegenski, not many researchers know that the German people had a somewhat similar system, and that it was also used in America from the 1700's to the early 1800's. They followed the practice of adding the letters "in" to a last name, thus: Bower (masculine), Bowerin (feminine); Mueller—Muellerin. The letters "er," of course, formed a common German ending, which adds to difficulty in research.

For instance, I have a photostated copy of the birth certificate of my Mother's Grandfather, Philip Pontius, born in 1826. On this certificate, his mother's maiden name was written (in German) as "Elizabeth Roserin." Thinking I was all set to trace the Roserin family, I spent two years searching **Pennsylvania** records for the name, which from all indications should have appeared there. Results were absolutely nil. **Careful** perusal of various early Pennsylvania records did turn up the names of Rose and Roser—so I figured there must be **a logical** reason why Roserin didn't appear anywhere. (Census records gave Pennsylvania as Elizabeth's birthplace, around 1805).

Then I remembered the Polish system of name endings, and began an investigation that finally turned up **definite proof** supporting the fact that "in" was commonly used as the feminine form of German surnames, well into the nineteenth century. So—in spite of the fact that my great-great-Grandmother's name appeared on her son's beautiful, **Pennsylvania** Dutch, handpainted birth certificate as Roserin—the family name had actually been Roser (sometimes, simply written as Rose!)—and several other records were eventually found to substantiate this.

All of which goes to prove that if you don't have at least a few thoughts of your own, it's impossible to get to the next town from **here**!

"X" Marks Another Spot

Many old documents, such as wills, land sales, etc., are frequently found signed with an "X" at the bottom. This is usually construed to mean the person signing in this fashion was unable to write. However, this is not necessarily true. On some documents, at various times, no other signature than the "X" mark was necessary, and was the commonly accepted form of signifying the paper had been accepted as written, by the one so signing. Thus, sometimes a well educated person signed with the "X" mark.

The Pennsylvania Archives

A most important research tool is the "Pennsylvania Archives." Since so many of us had ancestors who passed through (and frequently settled for a while in) Pennsylvania, it behooves us to have at least a speaking acquaintance with these wonderful, informative volumes. Many libraries have them on the shelves—but the person who really knows how to use these books is definitely very unique.

First of all, the collection consists of a total of 138 books; they record a vast amount of early Pennsylvania information on official governmental proceedings, as well as legal and military records and other useful data. The books are published in ten series, with books in each series being numbered starting with Volume number I. Thus, we will find, for instance, a reference to: Series IV, Volume 2, page 224. Some books have no index, but this little nuisance is taken care of by the fact that many times the following series will have several volumes of an index to the series that precedes it. In a nutshell, the collection is set up like this:

Colonial Records: 16 volumes of Pennsylvania Provincial Minutes.

First Series: 12 volumes, Secretary of the Commonwealth papers.

Second Series: 19 volumes, church records, militia rolls, 1777 Minutes of the Board of War and Navy Board, etc. **Volume 6 contains marriage records on pages 285-310.** — 6th Series

Third Series: 30 volumes, land warrantees and taxables, Virginia claims to western Pennsylvania, donation lands information, and militia rolls. "Last Purchase" warrantys will be found in Volume 26, pages 701 to 905. **The last four volumes are an index to the preceding sixteen.**

Fourth Series: 12 volumes, consisting mostly of Governor's data.

Fifth Series: 8 volumes, consisting of muster rolls and military lists. **A complete index for this Fifth Series will be found in Volume 15 of the Sixth Series.**

Sixth Series: 15 volumes, containing military rolls from the Revolution to the War of 1812, etc., church records, estate inventories, and other varied items of much interest. **Volume 15 indexes the entire Fifth Series.**

Seventh Series: **5 volumes comprised entirely of the index of over one million names appearing in the Sixth Series.**

Eighth Series: 8 volumes giving data on the Province of Pennsylvania's House of Representatives. Reprinted from eighteenth century records.

Ninth Series: 10 volumes concerning the Division of Public Records.

The Continental Army, Revolutionary War

The Continental Army was composed of volunteers from the thirteen Colonies, who had enlisted for varying terms of service. Some enlisted for three months, some for six or twelve months—or for the duration of the war, which at that time was expected to be three years. These men were the backbone of Washington's army—the men who endured the seven long years of hardship throughout the war. They marched back and forth across the country as needed; the volunteers came from all states, and were known as the Continental "Line."

Washington tried his best to have the term of enlistment set at three years, but this didn't meet with popular reception because many of the men felt it was necessary for them to get back home every so often to help with the crop harvest, plowing or planting as the case might be. Since each individual man was responsible for the welfare of his own family—no governmental assistance was forthcoming in those days!—it is easy to see why the shorter term of enlistment remained customary. Many men, however, after a short stint of service, enlisted for further tours of duty, repeating the enlistment-return home-re-enlistment routine frequently.

Some men, of course, enlisted directly into the Continental Army without first serving in a State Militia. Lists of names are available from various sources, with those pensioned or receiving bounty land being found in the Hoyt Index previously mentioned. If no service record can be found in any of the books or microfilms consulted, it is possible to write the Adjutant General of some states, or the Department of Archives, at the state capitol. Heitman's "Historical Register," contains a list of officers who served in the Continental Army; many names will also be found in Saffell's "Revolutionary Record."

Those men who served only in the state militias, of course, will not be found in the Continental Army lists. No exact figures are available, but rolls indicate that between 231,000 and 250,000 men served in the Continental Army, with around 164,100 in the state militias. A considerable number of records have been lost, so even though one is positive a particular ancestor did serve, it's not always possible to unearth definite proof, and some records probably just never will be found. The National Archives and Records Service provides one of the most wonderful finding aids imaginable, however, and should definitely be consulted. Even if your veteran never received a pension, he still may be on records of the General Services Administration for a military record—or perhaps on the Bounty Land records. The advice in all cases is: keep on looking! And remember there's always more than one way around **any** barn.

This author spent two full years hunting a Revolutionary War service record on one particular South Carolina man. He was not on the pension rolls, apparently received no bounty land, did not appear in any records at the National Archives, nor on any State service list. Yet, several of his brothers served in the Revolution—and he was of proper age for service. Finally, a small, thin volume on the shelves of the library at Fort Wayne, Indiana, provided the necessary proof. The long title of the little book was: "Stub Entries to Indents Issued in Payment of Claims Against South Carolina Growing Out of the Revolution." It stated our man was "issued on June 13 (no year), four pounds, eight shillings and seven pence sterling for Sundries for Militia use as pr. account audited." This was the only notation ever found, but these few lines proved service and enabled one of his descendants to become a member of the National Society Daughters of the American Revolution.

The DAR members from many states have, through the years, compiled books containing names of Revolutionary War soldiers buried in their state. This can provide valuable help for any researcher.

Many books have been printed containing names and other bits of information concerning soldiers who served in the

Revolution from that particular state. Included are the states of: Connecticut, Delaware, Georgia, Kentucky, Maine, Maryland, Massachusetts, New Hampshire, New Jersey, New York, North Carolina, Pennsylvania, Rhode Island, South Carolina, Tennessee, Vermont and Virginia. New information is constantly being found and published. The "DAR Patriot Index" will supply names of all Revolutionary War men or women whose descendants have been admitted to membership in the Daughters of the American Revolution, National Society.

Sending Money to Foreign Countries

There are three ways of sending money by mail to foreign countries, which is sometimes necessary if research is being conducted there. Just as most of us wouldn't have much use for money sent from Lower Slobovia, so—much as WE like it—people in other countries would have a hard time trying to pass our money at their own corner store.

The first method for sending money is by International Money Orders, obtained at any Post Office. These are much like our United States postal money orders, and may be used for sending amounts up to one hundred dollars.

The second method is by an American Express Company money order.

The third method is by a New York Bank draft, which may be purchased at any bank. Charges for all of these run quite small, with the International Money Order probably being a bit more costly than the other two.

To provide postage for a reply from any foreign country (which of course would find our United States postage useless) International Reply coupons should be purchased at any post office, then enclosed in a self addressed envelope, within your letter. The foreign recipient then exchanges these coupons at his own Post Office for postage necessary to send an answer back.

Then What Happens?????

One of the big problems that pile up in research is the question of what to do with all the material collected. Various methods have been devised to keep everything in order, but most people eventually work out their own technique. Obviously, what works for one, will not be particularly easy or helpful for another. Some methods are so complicated it would take six attorneys and three vice-presidents to figure them out. So—to each his own!

When huge quantities of unearthed material eventually collect, things can often get pretty complicated. And, even if you have more or less of a filing system, you're sure to some day be confronted with the darling little problem of where a certain piece of information should be filed—or, once filed, where to find it! Things can get mighty discouraging along about this time, unless you have an ace-in-the hole.

My own ace-in-the-hole happens to be manila folders— the plain, simple variety with no fancy pockets or ties. (These also happen to be the cheapest variety, which may be deemed another point in their favor!) When going to the library I take a large, loose-leaf notebook with plenty of lined pages in it. Tabs marking various family lines are very helpful, also. Being loose leafed, the book is easy to re-arrange at any time. Be sure the paper is the large 8½x11 size—this is no time to have to crowd copied information.

As material is found, it is written in the proper section of the notebook. Source notation must always be included, whether data is abstracted (pertinent information picked out from the whole), or quoted in full to support statements. Nothing—absolutely nothing!—can be more frustrating than to go many miles to a good library, spend the day researching, then upon reaching home discover you forgot to note a book title, author or page!

Upon arriving home from a trip to any library I usually try to type all my material on other paper, then place it in one of the manila folders which has been marked with the corresponding surname. This allows me to keep original notes in the loose leaf note book for further reference, if needed, yet also file each bit of new information with what has also been collected for that particular family.

The nicest part about these folders is that all those little bits of hastily scrawled morsels can be quickly chucked to a comfortable place of repose, when necessary. This way I at least know where they are— and if it takes me three months to get around to checking them over, all is still safe and sound. (In the beginning I lost far too much time shuffling through stacks of data on my desk, in twelve drawers and two closets— to say nothing of all the odd scraps I'd sometimes stash away under davenport cushions and dresser doilies—trying to remember where I had filed a particularly delectable bit of information!) Sometimes so much material accumulates in one folder that I have to start a second one on the same family. I keep every bit of correspondence on each family, too, so things sometimes can tend to get quite voluminous!

A small metal file box costing around three dollars (or whatever fantastic heights our inflationary economy eventually soars to!) will usually suffice as a depository for your manila folders and their precious contents. If you do quite a lot of research, you'll no doubt eventually have to graduate to at least a two-drawer file cabinet. This, in itself, will prove a real boost in your opinion of yourself as a researcher!

All sorts of things can be filed, including photocopies of pension applications, wills, vital records, lawsuits, family photographs, and so on, as the compiler wishes. At first you'll probably have to prop up the three or four folders with empty boxes, wadded-up paper towels, etc., but time has a way of remedying this state of affairs mighty quickly—and before you know it, you'll run out of room again!

Always be generous and gracious about sharing your information—remember that bread scattered upon the waters sometimes has a remarkable way of coming back to you as cake—occasionally even with icing on it!

Be sure to keep carbon copies of all letters you sent— they'll come in mighty handy more often than you might imagine.

Keep in mind: years ago it was customary to give the nearest large town as birthplace or place of residence. The idea behind this was that when moving to any new locality most people would be familiar with, say, Harrisburg, Plymouth, New York, and so forth. Very often, however, the actual locality was as much as one or two hundred miles from the particular town mentioned.

Thoughts on Lineage Research

My Grandpa was the nicest man
Who ever drew a breath of air;
He came from good and simple folks
Whose lives were bright and fair—

And they, in turn, descended from
Identically the same
Well-bred and ordinary type
Of gentleman and dame.

No trace of scandal ever touched
My Grandpa or his kin—
No sordid, underhanded deeds
Were they included in;

Each lived—then passed to his reward
Within the starry skies—
And not a single bit of sin
Had **ever** touched their lives.

But constantly I wish there **had**—
For I'm left in the lurch—
And records on some **nasty** folks
Would surely help research!

—Prudence Groff Michael

Commonly Used Words

Abstract—summary of important points in wills, etc.
abt.—about

Administrator—One appointed by the court to administer estate of deceased person

Acadia—the original name of Nova Scotia

Attest—to affirm or bear witness

Banns—published notice of intended marriage. Were frequently tacked on church doors, or read three successive Sundays by minister

Bounty—payment by city or town to volunteers when locality was asked by government to furnish quota of men during war

Blwt.—Bounty land warrant

bur.—buried or burial

C.—copyright

c., or ca.—Circa. (Latin for about)

Cadastral Survey—a public land survey recording the location, value and ownership of real estate, used to set tax amounts

Certified copy—an exact copy of any record that has been attested to by a notary public as being correct

cf.—compare

Codicil—addition to a will, modifying it in some respect

Collateral ancestors—those who belong to the same ancestral stock, but not in one's own direct line of descent—such as Aunts, Uncles, etc.

Consanguinity—blood relationship of some degree. There are two classifications: Agnate—all relationship on paternal side of family; Cognate—all relationship on maternal side of family

consort—spouse (husband or wife)

decedent—deceased person

Denizen—an alien admitted to residence in a country, who was to receive all or part of the rights of citizenship

deposition—written testimony of a witness, which has been authenticated

Devisee (or legatee)—person to whom property is given through a will

Devisor—person who gives property through a will

dower—legal right acquired to husband's real estate by wife through marriage

desc.—descendant

Donee—person to whom a gift is made

doc.—document

d.s.p.—(Latin) decessit sine prole—died without issue

d.v.p.—(Latin) decessit vita patris—died in father's lifetime d.y.—died young

ed.—editor, edited, edition

e.g.—for example. (from the Latin exempli gratia)

emigrant—one who leaves a country to settle some other place

estate—real and personal property

et. ux.—(Latin) or et. uxor—and wife

et. al.—among others

f., ff.—following page; pages

Freeman—one who was given civil or political liberty after taking an oath to a government or church

Freemen—(in tax or other records)—unmarried men age 21 or over, free of family obligations, so taxed as single men. They were transferred to regular tax lists after marriage, thus a search of tax records year by year will show year of marriage

Friend—member of the Society of Friends, or Quakers

Gazeteer—geographical dictionary giving names and descriptions of locations

Grantee—person who receives grant

Grantor—person who makes a grant

Great Valley Road—a principal road starting in southwestern Pennsylvania, running through the Shenandoah Valley to Knoxville, Tennessee, then on to Huntsville, Alabama.

Holographic will—one made and signed by testator in his own handwriting

h.s.—(Latin)—here is buried

ibid.—in the same place (Latin: ibidem)

i.e.—(Latin: id est)—that is

Indenture—agreement in writing between two or more parties, which was then cut or torn in a jagged line, each party receiving one section that could later be matched. Frequently used when an apprentice was bound to service, or when money loans were involved

Inmate—descriptive term used in census records many times; denoted married persons, usually laborers and mechanics, who owned no property

Immigrant—one who comes into a new country and settles there

intestate—died without leaving a will

l., ll.—line, lines

loc. cit.—in the place cited (Latin: loco citato)

Liber—book in which public records are kept, such as wills, mortgages, etc.

ms., mss.—manuscript, manuscripts

M.G.—minister of the Gospel

N.B.—note well (Latin: nota bene)

n.d.—no date

Necrology—registry of deaths

nee—name born with; maiden name of married woman

N.S.—new style calendar (Gregorian)

Nuncupative will—oral declaration or statement made before witnesses in testator's last illness, then later put into writing

N.X.N.—no Christian name

op. cit.—in the place cited. (Latin: loco citato)

O.S.—old style calendar (Julian)

Obit.—died

Patent—document that transferred legal title of public or government lands. Transfer was made at a Land Office. Records cover bounty land warrants, donation lands, homestead applications, private land claims, purchased by either government script or money. Information therein includes applicant's place of residence, name, dates and so forth.

Pennsylvania Dutch—mostly people from France, Germany and Switzerland, who settled in certain areas of Pennsylvania, in close proximity to each other, then more or less blended into a whole

Pre-emption application—application to buy land at the minimum price, by a person already living on the unappropriated land

p., pp.—page, pages

Probate—process of officially establishing the authenticity or validity of a will or estate

q.v.—which see, whom see. (Latin: quod vide)

Redemptioner—person who sold his services for a period of years to pay his ship's passage. No stigma was ever attached to the transaction

Relict—widow or widower

sic.—thus, or so, as copied, inferring probably incorrect data of which the copier is aware. Sic is usually enclosed in brackets

sine die—without date

s.p.—without issue

Testator—person who died leaving a will

Tory—a resident of the American colonies who remained loyal to England during the Revolutionary War

Tract Book—an index to transactions concerned with Public Lands, listing individual ownership by range and township, thus making property easy to locate

ux., uxor, uxoris—wife

V.D.M.—Voluns Deis: Minister

vide—see

Warning Out Law—notice given to residents of less than three years in a town, who were destitute and apt to become the responsibility of the town for maintenance. (Frequently widows left with a family.) Such persons then usually returned to their former place of residence and no disgrace was involved

X—prefix for words beginning with "Christ"

xped—christened

Xr—Christopher

/ —slanted line across lower part of letter "p" in early records indicated omission of **ar** or **or**

    —An easy way to avoid confusion between the words "emigrate" and "immigrate," is that the letter "e" comes before "i." Thus, a person first has to leave a country (emigrate,) before he can enter another country as an immigrant.

* * * * *

In the United States, a representative of any foreign consulate is the best person to contact regarding availability and whereabouts of various genealogical records in his own country. You may address The Consul General, (of any country), Washington, D.C.; many of the large cities in the United States have foreign consuls in them, also.

* * * * *

Always, in requesting birth or death certificates, ask for photostats. Hand written copies may omit important information.

The Endword–or Backword

(Anyway, the LAST Word!)

And so we come to the end of this little book! Since hardly one person out of ten ever takes time to read a "Foreword" introduction to anything, this author has dispensed with that item (did you notice?) and in its place decided to add an "Endword," or "Backword."

By now you should have acquired all sorts of choice, little tidbits of information that were perfect strangers before you started page one of "Don't Cry Timber!" Of course it has been impossible to cover many, many subjects that are actually involved in research, but for a long time I've felt that a simple, easy-to-read-and-understand book was much needed to get people started on genealogical research for various lines of their own families. This fact was pointed up during the seven years it was my privilege to serve as chairman of the lineage research committee of Schuyler Colfax chapter, Daughters of the American Revolution, at South Bend, Indiana. Six years on the state DAR lineage research committee were followed by three years as state chairman of DAR membership commission. Fortunately the importance of detailed accuracy in all things was instilled during twenty years of work as a medical laboratory technician.

The main purpose of "Don't Cry Timber!" is to give basic understanding, smooth the way, and provide at least an acquaintance with aids for genealogical research. But the far bigger concept is that once these things are actually underway you will automatically provide your own momentum—and on your own power be able to dig out increasingly intricate and sophisticated means of research for answers to those nagging problems sure to come along.

Sometimes, as Henry Ford used to say: "We go forward without facts and we learn the facts as we go along." So it is with genealogical research: our minds expand, and work becomes even more enjoyable and rewarding.

Material for this book was compiled on sort of a weekly-demand basis, several years ago, following an invitation to start a genealogy course at the South Bend YWCA. My class in "The Techniques of Genealogical Research" proved extremely successful, and provided many people with the "know-how" and desire necessary to begin research on their own interesting family lines.

Demand increased, so other classes followed at Elkhart and Plymouth, Indiana—my "old home town." After that I joined the teaching staff of Indiana University, South Bend, Division of Continuing Education, as genealogical research instructor.

Research can become a wholly absorbing thing—even for those who swear up and down they haven't the slightest desire to find out anything about their early family. We broaden our own horizons by diligent, dedicated work—and so make our own contentment. Hard work might not always fill a heart with sunshine, but at least some of the rays are bound to be absorbed, and thus make for a better outlook on life in general. It is my hope this book will generate a greater appreciation for—and pride in—the past, thus making for greater pride in the future. It seems to be a law of nature that pride begets pride—and without this virtue an empty spot remains in our lives.

Carlyle so beautifully wrote, "One life; a little gleam of time between two eternities; no second chance for us forevermore." Our own lives and deeds are the vital bridge between the past of our ancestors and the future of our descendants, so let us make sure that bridge is strongly and wonderfully built, and structurally sound. Let it truly be a preserving link between the past and the future, over which the past can continue into the years that are to come.

Compile your records carefully; speed, in this department, certainly is not the most important ingredient—but exactness **is.** From the time I was a small child I can remember my Mother saying over and over (quoting her maternal Grandmother Margaret Grube Pontius), "If a thing is worth doing at all, it's worth doing well." (This was the same peppy little grandmother who, in the 1880's and 1890's, when it was customary to iron the long, black, cotton stockings of the day, used to toss her head and declare, "It's a poor leg that can't iron its own stocking!")

Great-Grandmother Margaret's wisdom about doing a thing well, always deeply impressed me— and I'll remember it all my life. So should you. Satisfaction and contentment will be your reward—forevermore!

"For where your treasure is, there will your heart be also."

— The End —

*2284-21
1981
5-05
C